NOAH'S ARK

Bible Stories, Poems and Prayers

SELECTED AND RETOLD BY
ANN PILLING

ILLUSTRATED BY
KADY MACDONALD DENTON

Kingfisher

For David and Lorna, Lydia and
Naomi, with much love   A.P.

For Gina Pollinger   K.M.D.

KINGFISHER
An imprint of Larousse plc
Elsley House, 24-30 Great Titchfield Street
London W1P 7AD

This paperback edition first published by Kingfisher 1996
2 4 6 8 10 9 7 5 3 1

Material in this edition was previously
published by Kingfisher in 1990 in *Before I Go to Sleep*

A CIP catalogue record for this book
is available from the British Library.

ISBN 0 7534 0005 7

Printed in Hong Kong

For permission to reproduce copyright material, acknowledgement and thanks
are due to HarperCollins Publishers Ltd for "O God, who made the small nest of
the wren" from *The Golden Cockerel Book of Morning Readings* by M.E. Rose;
The Reverend Peter Midwood for "A Swaledale Parish Prayer".
Extracts from the Authorized Version of the Bible (The King James Bible), the
rights in which are vested in the Crown, are reproduced by permission of the
Crown's Patentee, Cambride University Press. New English Bible copyright ©
Oxford Unversity Press and Cambridge University Press 1961, 1970.

Contents

Now thank we all our God
  With heart and hands and voices,
Who wondrous things hath done,
  In whom his world rejoices;
Who from our mother's arms
  Hath blessed us on our way
With countless gifts of love,
  And still is ours today.

M. Rinkart

DEAR FATHER, hear and bless
Thy beasts and singing birds,
And guard with tenderness
Small things that have no words.

GOD MAKES THE WORLD

In the beginning, God made the heaven and the earth. But at first the earth was shapeless and empty, and everything was covered with thick darkness.

So God said, "Let there be light!" And there was light.

God saw that it was good, so he separated it from the darkness. He called the light 'Day' and the darkness 'Night'.

Then God made the sky over the great waters that covered the earth, gathering them together in one place so that dry land appeared. And on this land he set plants and trees growing, and it all seemed very good.

Then lights were put in the sky like great lamps, the sun, the moon and the stars, to give us the seasons and to make night and day. Into the sea God put all kinds of fish, and birds to fly above them in the air. "Have young," he said to them all, "and fill this earth of mine to overflowing."

Then he said, "Let dry land be filled with animals, both large and small, those that walk and creep, and jump and run." And it all seemed very good indeed.

At last, God made Man himself, and Man was special, because he looked like God. He was so special he was put in charge of all the things that now filled the marvellous new world, the plants and the herbs, the trees and their fruits, the fish and the birds, and all the creeping, running, jumping things. And God blessed him.

"Rule the earth and its creatures which I have made," he said. "They are for you."

Then God looked all around and felt that creation was very good indeed. It had taken six long days to make it, so on the seventh day he rested.

And that is why the seventh day of the week is a holy day, because it is when God rested from all his work.

Genesis 1, 2.

Glad that I live am I,
  That the sky is blue;
Glad for the country lanes
  And the fall of dew.
After the sun the rain,
  After the rain the sun;

This is the way of life
  Till the work be done.
All that we need to do,
  Be we low or high,
Is to see that we grow
  Nearer the sky.

Lizette Woodworth Reese

O GOD, who made the small nest of the wren and the great sky of the stars, we thank thee that thou art in all things, great and small. AMEN

M. E. Rose

8

THE SNAKE IN THE GARDEN

The very first man that God ever made was called Adam and for him, in a place called Eden, he planted a most beautiful garden. It had four great rivers flowing through it, and flowers and trees of every kind. Two trees were special, the Tree of Life and the Tree of the Knowledge of Good and Evil, which grew right in the middle. "You may eat fruit from any of the trees," God said, "except from the Tree of the Knowledge of Good and Evil. If you do that, then you will die."

So Adam lived in Eden, ruling over its animals and giving them all names. But he was lonely, so God made a woman to live with him and share the garden. Her name was Eve.

One day an evil creature came slinking by and said to her slyly, "Did God really tell you not to eat from this special tree?"

"Yes," said Eve, "and if we eat from the Tree of the Knowledge of Good and Evil, or even touch its fruit, we will die."

"That's not true," the creature told her. "You won't die. God only said that because if you do eat from it, you will become like him, knowing both good and evil, as he does."

Then Eve, seeing how lovely the fruit was, and wanting to be wise like God, stretched out her hand, took the fruit and ate. And when Adam came he ate too.

In the cool of the evening God walked in his garden and came looking for them, but in their shame they had hidden away. So he called out to them and said, "Adam, Eve, did you eat fruit from the forbidden tree?"

"Eve gave it to me," answered the man.

"But it was that evil creature's fault," the woman explained. "He tricked me."

Then God said to the creature, "You will be punished for this. From now on you will be a snake that cannot walk upright, but can only crawl along the ground, and you shall eat nothing but dust." And the wretched snake slithered away.

Then he said to Adam and Eve, "I will not let you die, but from now on you must work, tilling the stony soil until it produces food for you to eat. It will be hard for you, my children, because it is full of weeds and thorns. But now that you have tasted of the Tree of the Knowledge of Good and Evil, you must leave this garden and live in the world." And they went sadly away.

Then God thought, "What if they should reach out and taste from the Tree of Life too? They would live for ever, then."

So, when he had cast them out of Eden, he put an angel there, and a flaming sword that turned this way and that, to guard the Tree of Life.

Genesis 2, 3.

DEAR LORD,
Thank you that I am sometimes strong,
*   help me when I am still weak;*
Thank you that I am sometimes wise,
*   help me when I am still foolish;*
Thank you that sometimes I have done well,
*   forgive me the times I have failed you;*
And teach me to serve you and your world
*   with love and faith and truth,*
*   with hope, grace, and good humour.* AMEN

A Swaledale Parish Prayer

God who made the earth,
    The air, the sky, the sea,
Who gave the light its birth,
    Careth for me.

God who made the grass,
    The flower, the fruit, the tree,
The day and night to pass,
    Careth for me.

God who made the sun,
    The moon, the stars, is he
Who, when life's clouds come on,
    Careth for me.

Sarah Betts Rhodes

THE ENORMOUS BOAT

Noah was a good man, and walked with God, but the rest of the people had become very wicked. God was sad, but he was angry too, so he decided to bring a great flood upon the earth. But he wanted to save Noah and his family.

"You must build a huge wooden boat," God told him. "You must make it long and wide and tall, and paint it with tar so that the water can't get in. When it is finished you must shut yourself inside with your family, and into it you must take a pair of all the animals in my Creation, so that when the flood has gone down they can have young, to fill the earth again."

So Noah and his wife and their three sons set to work and built an enormous boat, exactly as God had said, and when it

was finished the animals came in, two by two: great lumbering elephants and long-necked giraffes, prickly old hedgehogs and nervous little mice, even a couple of tumbling furry kittens. And in through the windows flew birds of every kind: sparrows and thrushes, the raven and the turtle dove. When everyone was safe inside, God shut up all the doors and windows very tight. Then the rain came.

It rained for forty days without stopping once, and the whole earth turned into one enormous sea, filling the valleys and covering the mountain tops. Everything on earth was swept away and drowned, all except Noah and his family and his animals, snug and warm inside the enormous boat.

The flood waters boiled and bubbled and raged but God did not forget Noah, and at last he made a huge wind that blew across the earth, quelling the floods so that they began to go down. Little by little it stopped raining altogether, mountain tops broke the surface of the water and Noah's huge boat came to rest on top of Mount Ararat.

When all was calm, Noah opened a window and sent a raven out to see what was happening. When, after a week, it had not returned, he sent out a dove. But it came back very disappointed because no trees had appeared yet, so there was nothing to sit on. A few days later he sent it off a second time and this time it came back with a fresh green olive leaf in its beak. Then Noah knew that the flood really was over. Through his windows he could actually see dry land.

When he came out of the boat he built an altar to God, burning incense upon it to say thank you to him, for sparing their lives. And when God smelled the sweet perfume, he was sorry he had brought the flood.

"I promise," he told Noah, "never to destroy my creation again. While the earth remains, seedtime and harvest, cold and heat, summer and winter, day and night, shall not cease."

As a special sign of this promise he put a rainbow in the sky.

"Whenever I see it," he said, "I will remember what I have said, never to bring a terrible flood ever again."

So Noah and his family and all the animals went back safely into the world, and had children, so that the earth was full of living creatures, just as it had been before.

Genesis 6–9.

LOOK UPON THE RAINBOW and praise him that made it;
Very beautiful it is in the brightness thereof.
It compasseth the heavens about with a glorious circle,
And the hands of the most high have bended it.

Ecclesiasticus 43, v.11–12.

The animals went in two by two,
    Hurrah! Hurrah!
The animals went in two by two,
The elephant and the kangaroo,
    And they all went into the ark
    For to get out of the rain.

The animals went in three by three,
    Hurrah! Hurrah!
The animals went in three by three,
The wasp, the ant and the bumble bee,
    And they all went into the ark
    For to get out of the rain.

The animals went in four by four
    Hurrah! Hurrah!
The animals went in four by four,
The great hippopotamus stuck in the door,
    And they all went into the ark
    For to get out of the rain.

The animals went in five by five
   Hurrah! Hurrah!
The animals went in five by five,
They warmed each other to keep alive,
   And they all went into the ark
   For to get out of the rain.

The animals went in six by six
   Hurrah! Hurrah!
The animals went in six by six,
They turned out the monkey because of his tricks,
   And they all went into the ark
   For to get out of the rain.

The animals went in seven by seven,
   Hurrah! Hurrah!
The animals went in seven by seven,
The little pig thought he was going to heaven,
   And they all went into the ark
   For to get out of the rain.

Traditional

19

THE BABY IN THE BASKET

Pharaoh, the King of Egypt, was very worried. The Israelites, who lived as slaves in his kingdom, seemed to be growing stronger and cleverer with every day that passed. "What if they rise up against me?" he said to himself. "What if they make war on my people and drive them all away?" So he worked out a cruel plan to get rid of them all.

The plan was this: every baby boy born to an Israelite woman was to be thrown into the river Nile. Nothing could live very long in there, because it was full of crocodiles.

But one woman, who came from the family of Levi, was determined to save her little son from Pharaoh. The baby was strong and healthy and for three whole months she managed to keep him hidden.

The time came, however, when she could not hide her precious secret any longer. Someone was bound to find out about the baby sooner or later, and when they did he would be killed. So she wove a little basket out of rushes, made a lid for it and daubed it all over with clay and tar, to stop the water coming in. She put the baby inside and hid the basket in the tall reeds at the edge of the river. Then she crept away. But her daughter Miriam hid in the shadows, just to see what would happen next.

Quite soon King Pharaoh's daughter came along for her morning bathe, while her maids walked up and down the bank. As she knelt down she saw the funny little rush basket hidden in the reeds, and she sent one of her servant girls to bring it out.

When they opened it up they found a baby lying there. He started to cry when he saw all the strange faces. "Why,

this is a Hebrew child," the princess said, "poor little soul." She felt very sorry for him.

Just then, Miriam stepped out of her hiding place. "Shall I find someone to look after the baby?" she said cleverly, "one of the Hebrew women, perhaps?"

"Yes," said Pharaoh's daughter. "Go and fetch someone, quickly." So Miriam ran home and brought her mother back to her own little son, snug in his basket of rushes.

"If you will look after this child for me," the princess told her, "I will pay you good wages." So his mother took her little son into her arms again, and carried him safely home.

When he was old enough, however, Pharaoh's daughter took him to live with her in the royal palace, and he became her adopted son. She called him Moses because the name means 'pulled out of the water'.

Moses grew up to be one of the greatest of all the Israelites, and it was he who led his people out of Egypt, where they had been slaves, back to the good land that God had always promised them, the land that overflowed with milk and honey.

Exodus 1, 2.

Hush, little baby, don't say a word,
Papa's gonna buy you a mocking bird.
If that mocking bird don't sing,
Papa's gonna buy you a diamond ring.
If that diamond ring turns to brass,
Papa's gonna buy you a looking glass.
If that looking glass gets broke,
Papa's gonna buy you a billy goat.
If that billy goat don't pull,
Papa's gonna buy you a cart and bull.
If that cart and bull turn over,
Papa's gonna buy you a dog named Rover.
If that dog named Rover don't bark,
Papa's gonna buy you a horse and cart.
If that horse and cart fall down,
You'll still be the sweetest little baby in town.

Traditional

CRADLE SONG

Sweet dreams, form a shade
O'er my lovely infant's head;
Sweet dreams of pleasant streams
By happy, silent, moony beams.

William Blake

FAITHFUL RUTH

Long ago there was a great famine in the land of Judah. A man called Elimelech, with his wife Naomi and their two sons, went to find food in a foreign country called Moab. While they were living there Elimelech died. Both the sons found wives for themselves. One was called Orpah and the other Ruth.

They lived in Moab for ten years, but then both the sons died too and old Naomi, left all alone, decided to go back to her own country of Judah. She had heard that God had blessed it with food again.

But she told Ruth and Orpah to go back to their own families. "You have been good to me," she said. "Now may God be good to you. May he bring you new husbands, and new homes." And she kissed them.

Then Ruth and Orpah wept bitterly. "Do not send us away," they pleaded. But Naomi was firm. "Go back to your own people," she said, "for I am an old woman now. I have no sons left to be your husbands."

So, very sadly, Orpah said goodbye, but Ruth clung to Naomi. "Do not ask me to leave you," she said, "for where you go I will go too, and where you stay I will stay. Your people shall be

my people, and your God my God. Nothing but death will part us now."

So Ruth and Naomi travelled on together until they reached Bethlehem, just as the barley harvest was beginning. Ruth went into the fields to follow the reapers, hoping to pick up a few ears of corn that had been left behind.

Now all the land round about belonged to a very rich man called Boaz. He noticed the foreign girl gathering corn in his field and he asked his reapers who she was. "She came from Moab," they told him, "with old Naomi. She's been here since day-break, following us round and picking up the stray ears of corn."

Then Boaz called Ruth over to him and told her to stay close to his servants. "If you're thirsty," he said, "drink some of the water they have brought."

"But why are you so kind to me?" she said in amazement. "I'm just a foreigner."

"I have heard how good you have been to Naomi," he told her, "how you left your own home to be with her, and came instead to a strange land. May the Lord reward you, Ruth, for what you have done, the Lord God of Israel under whose wings you have taken refuge."

When the reapers stopped to eat, he made sure she had food too. "Don't scold her," he whispered to them, "but let her go among the barley sheaves and gather grain. In fact, drop some in her path deliberately, so that she has plenty."

When she got home again, Ruth told Naomi all about Boaz's kindness. "Blessings on him," said the old woman thankfully. "This shows that God still remembers us and cares for us, even now, when all our loved ones are dead." Then she told Ruth to tell Boaz that he was a relation of Elimelech, her dead husband. "Perhaps he will give us more help," she said.

So Ruth went off to find him, and when he heard what Naomi had said he told her to hold her cloak out wide. Into it he poured a great measure of barley, and she put it on her back and went home to show Naomi. "I believe that Boaz will not rest until he has done even more for us," the old woman told her.

And she was right, because Boaz sent for Ruth, and asked her to be his wife. In time she bore him a son. "Blessed be the Lord today," she told Naomi joyfully, "he did not leave you alone. This grandson has come to give you new life, and comfort in your old age. And I, your daughter-in-law, who loved you so dearly, have done more for you in the end than all your sons!" Then Naomi took her little grandson, and held him very close.

The neighbouring women called the baby Obed, and he became the father of Jesse, who in turn became the father of King David. And it was from this great family that Jesus himself was born. That is why he was sometimes called 'the Son of David'.

Ruth 1—4.

AN OLD WOMAN OF THE ROADS

Oh, to have a little house!
    To own the hearth and stool and all!
The heaped-up sods upon the fire,
    The pile of turf against the wall.

To have a clock with weights and chains
    And pendulum swinging up and down,
A dresser filled with shining delph,*
    Speckled and white and blue and brown.

I could be busy all the day
    Clearing and sweeping hearth and floor,
And fixing on their shelf again
    My blue and white and speckled store.

I could be quiet there at night,
    Beside the fire and by myself,
Sure of a bed, and loth to leave
    The ticking clock and the shining delph.

Och! but I'm weary of mist and dark,
    And roads where there's never a house or bush,
And tired I am of bog and road,
    And the crying wind and the lonesome hush.

And I am praying to God on high,
    And I am praying him night and day,
For a little house, a house of my own –
    Out of the wind's and the rain's way.

*pottery   *Padraic Colum*

MAY THE ROAD rise to meet you,
May the wind be always at your back,
May the sun shine warm on your face,
The rain fall softly on your fields;
And until we meet again,
May God hold you in the palm of his hand.

A Gaelic Blessing, from Ireland

THE BOY WHO KILLED A GIANT

David was a shepherd boy, the youngest son of a man called Jesse. He was handsome and strong, and he was brave too, for wild animals had come prowling round his flocks at night, and David had killed them with his bare hands. He could also play wonderful tunes on his harp, and when King Saul had wild and terrible dreams, he would send for David so that the boy might sing songs to him. The soft, sweet music always sent the king to sleep. Saul loved David very much, and though he was just a shepherd, he became the king's special armour-bearer too.

Now King Saul and his Israelites had been fighting a long fierce war with the Philistines, and once more the two armies were facing each other, this time across a deep valley. From the Philistines' camp strode a huge man called Goliath. He wore a massive bronze helmet and a clanking coat of chain mail, and his spear was as thick as a great tree trunk.

"Send a man out to fight me!" he bellowed. "If I kill him, you will all become our slaves!" At the sound of his voice the

Israelites all quaked in terror; no one dared move an inch.

Morning and evening, for forty days, Goliath came and jeered at the terrified soldiers. David, who was up in the mountains looking after his father's sheep, heard about it and secretly wondered what to do. Then his father Jesse gave him some food to take to his brothers who were soldiers in King Saul's army. While he was talking to them Goliath appeared yet again.

"Come and fight!" he yelled. But all the Israelites ran away.

David alone knew that God was on their side, and he told the king that he would fight the giant himself.

"Oh no," Saul said in dismay. "He is a great warrior and you are a mere boy."

But David answered, "The God who saved me from the lion and the bear will surely save me from Goliath." When he heard this the king said, "Go, and may the Lord be with you," and he gave David armour, a coat of mail, a helmet and a sword.

Everything was so heavy that the boy could hardly walk so he took it all off, picked up his shepherd's crook instead, and chose five smooth pebbles from the bed of the stream. He tucked them into his knapsack with his little leather sling, then he set off to meet the giant. Goliath sneered horribly when he saw a young boy approaching. "Am I a dog," he screamed, "that you bring nothing but sticks to beat me with? Come on then, I'll soon finish you off, and when you're dead I'll feed your body to the crows."

But David replied, "You may have a spear and a javelin but I have the power of Almighty God, the Lord, the one on whom you have turned your back. Goliath, it is you who will die today, that all the earth may know that there is a God in Israel."

As the giant rushed upon him, David took one of his little pebbles, fitted it into the sling and fired it straight at Goliath's forehead. It struck him so hard that it sank deep into the flesh and the huge man was soon rolling dead at David's feet.

And from that day on David lived in the royal palace and became the special friend of Jonathan, the king's son. And Jonathan loved him as he loved his own soul.

1 Samuel 16, 17.

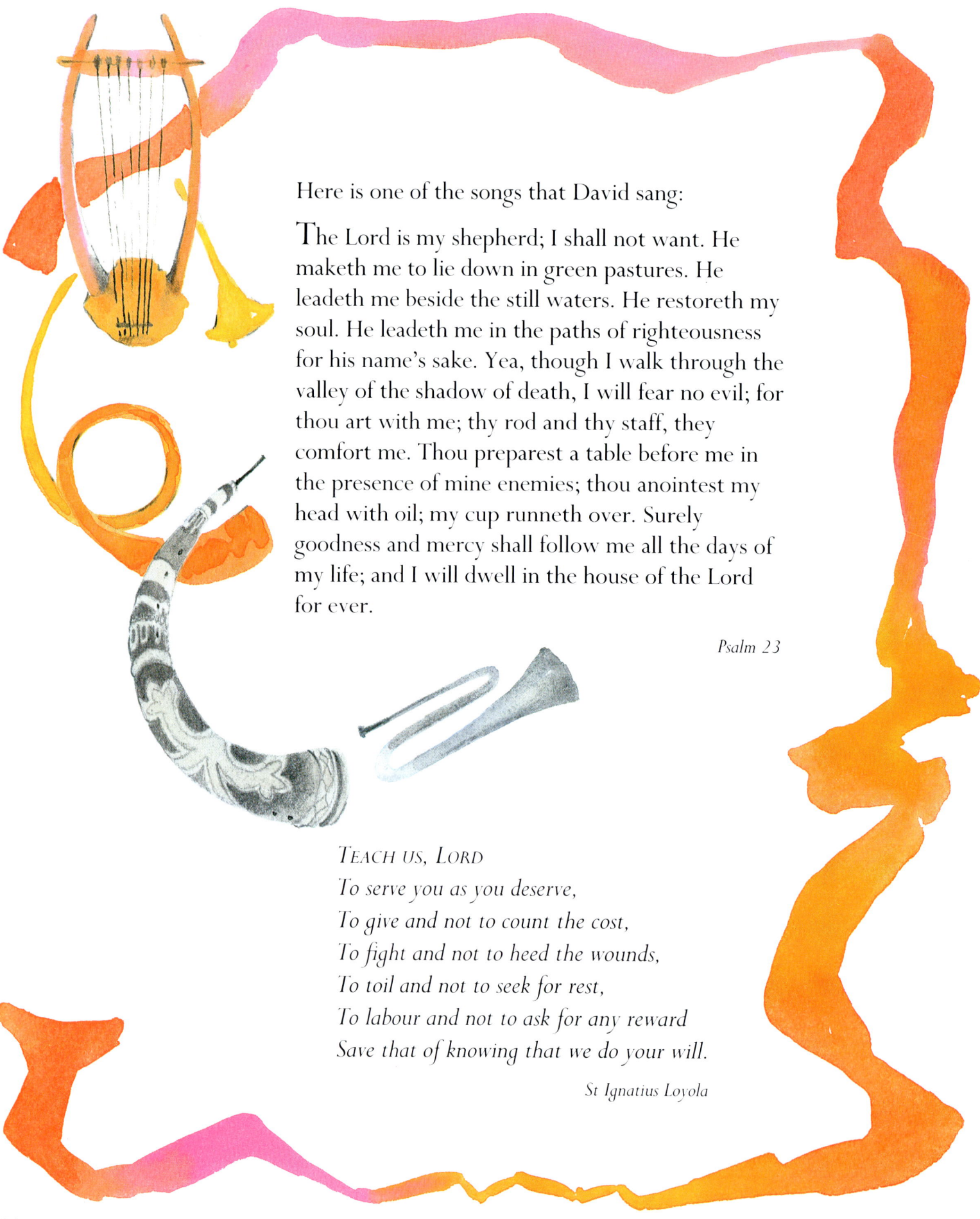

Here is one of the songs that David sang:

The Lord is my shepherd; I shall not want. He maketh me to lie down in green pastures. He leadeth me beside the still waters. He restoreth my soul. He leadeth me in the paths of righteousness for his name's sake. Yea, though I walk through the valley of the shadow of death, I will fear no evil; for thou art with me; thy rod and thy staff, they comfort me. Thou preparest a table before me in the presence of mine enemies; thou anointest my head with oil; my cup runneth over. Surely goodness and mercy shall follow me all the days of my life; and I will dwell in the house of the Lord for ever.

Psalm 23

TEACH US, LORD
To serve you as you deserve,
To give and not to count the cost,
To fight and not to heed the wounds,
To toil and not to seek for rest,
To labour and not to ask for any reward
Save that of knowing that we do your will.

St Ignatius Loyola

THE AMAZING FLOUR BARREL

Elijah was a holy man from Gilead and God had given him a very special gift; he was able to look into the future, and see what was going to happen.

One day, in a dream, he saw that the rain would stop falling for months on end, and that there would be a terrible famine. Then he heard the voice of God telling him to prepare for a very long journey. "Go east," said the voice, "until you find a little stream that flows near the River Jordan. It will provide water for you to drink, and I have commanded ravens to bring you food."

So Elijah did what God had said. He found the little stream and drank from it, and sure enough, each morning and evening the ravens carried food down to him in their beaks.

But in the end even the little stream dried up, and Elijah became very thirsty. "Now go to the city of Zarephath," God commanded. "There is a woman living there who will look after you." So Elijah set off again and came at last to the gate of the city where he saw a poor woman gathering a few sticks to make a fire.

"Could you bring me some water?" he asked her, "and a little food? I have walked so many miles today." But the woman said bitterly, "I have hardly any food left, only a handful of flour in a barrel, and a tiny drop of oil in a jar. These sticks are to make the fire for my very last meal. When that's gone I shall die, and so will my poor son."

"Don't be afraid," Elijah told her. "Go home and make your fire. But when the food is cooked bring me a little too. God has promised that your barrel of flour and your jar of oil will never be empty, not until it rains again."

So she went home and did exactly what he had told her. And it was true; there was always oil in the jar and flour in the barrel. God had kept his word.

But even though they now had enough to eat, her son fell ill, wasted away, and died. In her grief the poor woman turned on Elijah, the stranger. She blamed him. "Why did you bring this on me?" she wept. "Did you simply come here to remind me of the mistakes I've made in my life, and to punish me for them?"

Very patiently, Elijah gathered the boy in his arms, took him upstairs and laid him on his own bed. Then he prayed to God, long and hard. "Why has this awful thing happened," he said, "to a poor woman who took me in, and looked after me? Dear Lord, bring her child to life again, I beg you."

And God heard his prayer. Very soon the boy started to breathe again, opened his eyes and sat up. Elijah took him down to his mother. "He is alive," he said.

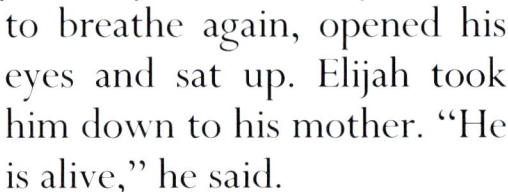

Then the woman held her son very tight. "Now I know you are a true man of God," she said joyfully, "a special person through whom he shows his power and his love." Through Elijah, God had turned her darkness into light.

I Kings 17.

LORD, make me an instrument of your peace.
Where there is hatred, let me sow love,
Where there is injury, pardon,
Where there is despair, hope,
Where there is darkness, light,
Where there is sadness, joy.

St Francis of Assisi

THE FRIENDLY LIONS

In the days of King Darius there was a man in his court called Daniel. He was a fine man who walked with God, and the king liked and trusted him. He was planning to put him in charge of the whole kingdom. But the royal servants were deeply jealous and they were watching Daniel very carefully.

Their problem was that Daniel did nothing wrong at all, and they soon realized that the only way to get him into trouble was to make a new law to trap him. They knew he was a very holy man, and faithful to his God, so they wrote out a special decree which said that from now on people could only pray to the king. Anybody who disobeyed would be thrown into a pit full of lions.

Now Daniel heard about this new law, but he took no notice. Three times a day he went off to his house, opened the windows so that he could look towards Jerusalem, fell on his knees and prayed. The jealous servants spied on him, then rushed off to tell the king what they had seen. "Doesn't the new law say that prayers may only be offered to you," they said slyly, "and that anyone who disobeys must be thrown to the lions?"

"It is true," admitted King Darius, though his heart was heavy. "It does say that, and a royal law cannot be changed."

"Well, Daniel is taking no notice," they informed him. "He prays to God three times a day. We've seen him."

When the king heard this he was very unhappy, because he loved and honoured Daniel, and all day he thought hard for some way to save him. But the jealous servants came back again and told him firmly that the new law could not be changed.

So Darius gave orders for Daniel to be thrown to the lions. "But may your God, whom you serve so faithfully, save you now," he said, as Daniel was dragged away from the palace to the deep pit where the savage creatures were waiting.

The servants rolled a huge stone over the entrance and the king came and marked it with his own special

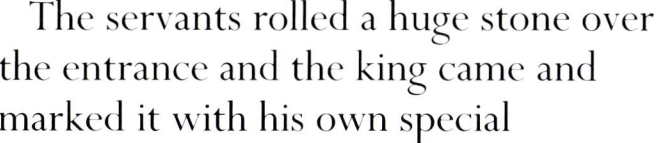

ring, to show that nobody must break in. Then he went back to his palace. For the rest of the day he neither ate nor drank, and he sent away his court musicians. All night he lay tossing and turning, and thinking about Daniel.

In the morning he woke very early, ran to the pit and called out in fear, "Daniel, servant of the living God, has the one whom you served so faithfully been able to save you from the jaws of the lions?"

And from deep in the pit a voice rang out. "O King," it said, "may you live for ever. In the night, God sent his angel to shut the lions' mouths. He knew I was innocent, and that I had done you no harm."

Darius was overjoyed to hear him and he ordered his men to bring Daniel up out of the pit. They could find no marks on his body at all. That was because he had trusted in God with his whole heart to save him.

As for the jealous servants, who had tricked him and tried to have him killed, they were thrown into the pit themselves. Even before they had reached the bottom all the lions sprang up, and devoured them whole.

And the king wrote a grand decree, for every nation upon earth, bidding all people to fear and honour Daniel's God. "For he is the living God," he said. "He delivered my dear servant Daniel from the lions' jaws, and his Kingdom shall last for ever and ever."

Daniel 6.

38

OUT OF THE PIT

I waited patiently for the Lord;
He bent down to me, and heard my cry.
He brought me up, out of the muddy pit,
Out of the clay and the quicksand,
And set my feet upon a rock.
He has put a new song in my mouth,
A song of praise to our God.

from Psalm 40

DEAR LORD, You have done such wonderful things.
You looked after Daniel, and I know you will
look after me. AMEN

Ann Pilling

In peace I will lie down and sleep,
For you alone, Lord, make me dwell in safety.

Psalm 4, v.8.